ordsmithery*

CW00419657

fire in the head

sm jenkin

First published in 2018 by
Wordsmithery
5 Curzon Road
Chatham
Kent, ME4 5ST
www.wordsmithery.info

isbn 978-0-9926853-9-3
printed in Great Britain on recycled paper
by Inky Little Fingers

contents

foreword

So here it is, the poetry book that I was never going to write. But then

> *I went out to the hazel wood,*
> *Because a fire was in my head*

When I was growing up, Medway wasn't the kind of place that valued poetry. It didn't have much of a history that I could see either. It wasn't until after I'd left and came back that I learned better, and became embarrassed at my ignorance. The Medway teems with words, music and a fascinating and varied history that's not acknowledged in polite company. This includes the stories of people like my mum and dad who worked at the Dockyard and the (naval) hospital. I write to remember them. They made the place we live in and shaped the people who live here now, even if we don't fully remember how.

I still didn't like poetry until I tried it at an evening class run by Medway's own Phil Kane. So I started to like writing, but still felt self-conscious about it. What right did I have to even try? He introduced me to the history of the Medway Poets, to the guys at Urban Fox, to my friends who would go on to found the Medway Mermaids writing group. So it seemed like poetry could be written by anyone, even someone like me. Could say something meaningful, even to someone like me. So when I met Sam and Barry Fentiman-Hall of Wordsmithery I was ready to take part in the various projects that have blossomed since then. Thank you Phil, Sam and Barry, you've done so much to nurture new writers in Medway.

The title of this book *Fire in the Head* comes from the poem 'The Song of Wandering Aengus' by W.B. Yeats. It is the best description of poetic inspiration that I have come across, that mysterious and addictive process that can consume you.

There are many more writers and histories for you to discover, some older than others but all worth hearing. How about you start at your local library or archives service – they're pretty cool there.

Medway Mermaid

You've probably heard about my flowing
hair. And my silvery scales. But
has anyone ever told you about my
teeth, my darling?
My mother was mated with a great
white. She says; *He tracked me out on the coral
reef.* My lips trace the gash in her
belly; ask no questions. *It brought me
you,* she says. She says; *you chewed your
way out.* That's why I'm here on this rock, neither
fish nor fowl.
I can look after myself, darling. I don't
need you to protect me;
when mermaids smile, we
bare our teeth.

Aspiration between lines

They came for us then, at
about the second or third year.
Brave young lads in uniforms
pressed at a cool 90° angle,
protractor sharp
old enough to admire,
young enough to laugh with.
The cold dead things laid out
on the trestle tables
after lunch.
Pick this one.
Feel the curve in your palm.
They were smart enough
to leave the ammunition back at
Brompton Barracks.

The King's men
recruited their maths
boys over in Rochester,
building bridges
far enough out.
The squaddies came
our way, across the
field of fire
comprehensive in their
breach and clear.
And us with our
brothers on the dole,
aspiring brickies, chippies
painters, handy at nothing.
What was it for us

after that?
Double history,
the penned pictures of navvies
staring back, from between two
blue textbook covers
at us, scribbling between
the Great Lines.

Dolomite King

and so again
this moment monumental
at this monument to pain
at this dumb show and tell
at this, marble veined
and flat out blank

tombstones more eloquent
than this, sharp edged
curve that needs a
chisel or razor or some
other driven blade,
chivvied along to
strike out
some sense
some words
some thing

and so again
this dolomite king
this refractive, redactive
king of the corals,
live shells cooked,
snails remade
courtesy of the folded
heft of the world

this moment monumental
this monument to pain
some dumb show and tell
some marble veins stay
flat out blank
you fill the gaps

Life on Chatham

Alone on the 101 bus, my mother's ghost beside me,
framed by dusty tide-marked windows, steady Wi-Fi signals
as we pass freshly painted gates, open from 10 till 6
and the mute cannons supine beneath the royal crest

framed by dusty tide-marked windows, steady Wi-Fi signals
following trails of dockyard grime, buried under maps and heritage signs
and the mute cannons supine beneath the royal crest
I remember my father's footprint; crowned with dust on the bus floor

following trails of dockyard grime, buried under maps and heritage signs
It looked alien, alone, like it had rocked in from outer space
I remember my father's footprint; crowned with dust on the bus floor
I'd seen many like it leading away from our front door

It looked alien, alone, like it had rocked in from outer space
a delicate pattern to decipher; concrete proof that he had been here;
I'd seen many like it leading away from our front door
My mother knew it best, knew that it was his. Saw

a delicate pattern to decipher, concrete proof that he had been here;
our small beginnings of a monument, now just add sand and water.
My mother knew it best, knew that it was his. Saw
where their stories lie unmarked, long laid to rest

our small beginnings of a monument, now just add sand and water.
Sailing by the historic dockyard, the white trimmed Admiral's office
where their stories lie unmarked, long laid to rest
the hearts of oak fossilised before our feet

Sailing by the historic dockyard, the white trimmed Admiral's office
alone on the 101 bus, my mother's ghost beside me,
the hearts of oak fossilised before our feet
as we pass freshly painted gates, open from 10 till 6

Static sails

Static sails
spotted
sailing across
showers of rain,
shining in the
sun's rays slipping out from
silent sodden clouds. A
singular sail
sheltered in the
shade of cream furnishings,
softened long ago by spit'n'
spindrift

sealed in its sanctuary,
sitting and seamlessly blending into
shadows, the
solitary boat
slowly stockpiling dust,
stays silent. But
still? She dreams and,
slowly

spread my dreams with her
standing, in the doorway opposite
sinking deep into temporary
sanctuary,
safely anchored in
sediment.
She sits tight until the
streams and tides drift back, and I'll
sashay along the current with her;
So long

Nordkapp

Response to 'The Road Not Taken' by Robert Frost

The first night aboard, after the announcements made
in Norwegian, Dutch, then English – I gather the
courage to ask what to do if I fall. Even this close to
Bergen, it is clear that the journey between inky grey waves

is a one-way trip. There is no hurry to embark, I know that
route well. Need only follow again the imprint of
your boot, the painkillers scattered like breadcrumbs
beneath an empty stairwell.
Instead, I choose another path to the end of the world.

Beside the caged globe at the northern cape, at the
mixing point of the Norwegian and the Barents Sea, flows
the river that cannot be stepped into twice. This is
not the same water Steven Borough traversed;
I am not the same who stepped onto this boat a week ago.

I have seen between the bars, looked out above the
frozen crests, where icebergs of sun shatter and bounce,
fall; follow the snow lining the water's limits down,
draping the sharp angled blank whiteness
in strips of orange peel, candy-floss pink and
baby blue.

Blue tinged anchor

In moments of doubt, the
blue-tinged anchor on your
upper arm wanders close
to your wrist.
Or was it your bicep?
No that was the swallow, wasn't it?
A swallow was there,
a navy-blue swallow.
Scorched somehow by the
tropical sun that never
saw past your wrists,
not since my school's Lilt-tinged
sports days.
Those sunned days at the dockyard
faded it, perhaps. Chatham could be
fierce hot back then,
hot enough to melt the heels of
your shoes.
Or was it from one of those
stop-overs at some bar,
where thirsty merchant
seamen satisfied their tongues.

To thee belongs the rural reign,
Rule Britannia! Rule the waves.
Then home again;
a comb-over for a king
of the subs, a golden cup of special
to toast the merchant man, and
his medals gathering dust
at your wife's bedside cabinet.
Too late to ask you now
what they were all for.
They lie there now
inside the fake book,
at the base near where the
broken bedside light flickered,
where the black turn dial radio
received static;
where my mother sleeps alone.

Swimming the North Downs

As if Job's whale
were waiting
above the trees,
grey mouth tight
lipped against the
unspoken rain.

And clouds of rape
splash yellow above
poppied grass,
root deep in beached
bones of plankton
condensing along the
swell of the memory
of ice,
melting the
mineral rock layers
down the gradient
and out at the
softened gap of her
dressed in purple foxglove
and flint edged nettle.

Anne Pratt

Everything is illuminated, the beauty in the details
of what is; Traveller's Joy, Enchanter's
Nightshade, Gold of Pleasure fractured ferns.
All eloquent with their own
language; splendour laid out for one
who takes the time to discern.

But the spectator casts a shadow; perception
is deception. A self-taught illustrator
could conjure anything.
Beware the mote in your eye,
madam. Stand aside for the
real scientists; observe.

Blue throated warblers, Robins, Blackbirds.
Our Native Songsters calling out from
layered plates, imprinted with coloured
stones. Her chromomania pages sold out anyway,
migrating along steely railtrack routes, illuminated
by lamps nestled in unnumbered parlours.

Anne Pratt, a successful self-taught botanical illustrator, was
born in Strood in 1806. She grew up in Chatham, and was
taught at the Eastgate House School in Rochester.

Spring Famished Green

I am famished for green,
parched, the kind of hunger
banked and burning that
combusts at the end of your tongue

I am famished for green,
the kind that carves into your
bleached red gut, roots and
branches out through your chest

I am famished for green,
the kind that breaks the end of
old dead branches, leaps out
and calls itself to itself

I am famished for soft green
leaves, that end the fast I had not
known I had entered.

Cordyline sunbathing

This morning, as the
world curled away from
the rest of it all, the sun's
light crawled brokenly over
vicious frosted spikes.

Purple cordyline
bruised into
ice-peaked focus,
the shattered pink air
pinned below
serrated clouds,
below power lines
humming alongside
car exhausts.

A police siren
bleeds into the distance.

Only a fool

It is the fool who curls up into the
shifting mulchy tides –
don't you know that you are sleeping
above a deadline?

It is the fool who curls up into the
ticking path of the kernel –
don't you know that you are about to
explode into a blossom?

It is the fool who curls up
after the blossoming –
don't you know that you are what
we have been waiting for?

Lesser Short-toed Lark

Ambiguity confuses me;
give me rules, the
clear delineation between
Earth and Sky,
let me see my way,
from the solidity beneath and
between my claws,
before I let loose.

At a distance I am
brown and unremarkable,
but
hear my chorus –
short, varied, succinct –
my breast is plastered with
go-faster stripes.
Compared to the short-toed
lark, I'm a bit of a dark horse.
But not 'lesser', rather;
'Exclusive'

Chicken feed

To be well adjusted to the world
is like twisting the neck of a chicken,
and calling yourself an Osteopath.
Bertram's sun will not now rise for you –
and the world twists and sinks
and brings you with it into shadow.

To be well adjusted to the world
is to be an apology on the tip of the beak
of that chicken. The dumb seeds scattered
on the dirt will not now rise for you –
and the world twists and sinks
and brings you with it into shadow.

To be well adjusted to the world
is to have your neck snapped like
that chicken, wondering
why it hangs at an odd angle,
until your wings are out of sight,
they will not now rise for you –
and the world twists and sinks
and brings you with it into shadow.

To be well adjusted too,
the world twists and sinks
and follows you into the shadow.

Mechanic flying fury

White silk scarf braided around
his young neck, James McCudden
frowns into the clockworked metal;
nestled in the tail of his
Royal Aircraft Factory S.E.5a,
this protection necessary
5000 feet below his
comfort zone.

Up there he can breathe;
it is easier to see
defensive possibilities,
an angle of attack,
the other chap.
Heroism has a method;
requires thought and
careful planning.

On departure,
he wraps his medals in a plain
brown envelope for his sister.
Ballast is not necessary
for this trip.

*James McCudden, a gifted pilot and a skilled
mechanic during World War 1, was born in
Brompton in 1895. He died in July 1918.*

Casting Cobham's Shade

At the turn of the Weald,
Cobham's unconsecrated pyramid
shimmers beneath the grime,
a circle squared into immortality,
the empty tomb
a step and a step
away from the diminishing
yews, where the
fifth earl fell.

Dorset stone curves,
Doric arches and Greek columns
sheltering pristine black French
marble, beside angular masonic
fish swimming in an echo bath,
within a field of coppiced metal spears.

His Hands

On a day like this,
you bring flowers, but
he is without.
I remember those hands
holding things,
holding the electric drill as he
spat onto the concrete,
to cool the white-hot tip
before lacing the wire fence.
Holding nails in one hand, a golden can
of Special Brew in the other,
Claddagh ring glinting in its shadow.

But never nothing.
Never so cold and still.
His swallow tattoo, fading
so far from the sea,
covered with his smart grey suit
and white shirt,
like the kind he wore the day he
married my mother.

Our lady of Gillingham
is expecting him.
You'd think he'd have
remembered
the flowers.

Dandelion: a declaration

An orange signal-flare
explodes above splintered grass;
Crisp ambition glares out from
bellicose spikes; my
boundaries are clear and
sharp

a brittle stalk, strong but light,
braced securely above the sea of
gossamer ferns and bright-faced
impostors;
this is mine; within this circle,
my space, my
own

lop off my head and another grows, my
roots are strong and reach far;
poison cannot hurt me, nor spades unearth,
my tongue defended by *dent de lion*,
the lion's teeth of Brighid;
Goddess of words, smithcraft and
healing.
You will remember me.

Capel Fleet

where farmer's soiled edges
dissolve into the clear light
of earth-tones mixed into
a watercolour water pot,
basking towards a still life
blue-grey reflection of clouds,
winter's soft feathered plumage
spiked by sharp edged reeds.
Sucking at salted waters,
the sticky underside of a rogue
cow's tongue, and in that moment's
distraction you missed
the first steps
of a dancing cloud, a
murmuration of starlings
free spinning into waves

here now tears open the
water's rapturous embrace, at the
soft green landing place between
the burning Arctic ices and
distant heated sands;
with gold pointed precision,
falls the Peregrine Falcon
free diver into the skywaters,
making good before
ice-white easterlies bring in the
rough-legged buzzards,
hovering over
salted waterways,
spiked by sharp edged
reeds.

GD and the Narwal

Who were you GD?
Your name spirals from the
top of the Turks' head, edges twined
sensuously into the narwhal's tooth
with such regular precision;
each knot tightly wound before
the finish, three inches from the ground.

She's aged well, for all her travels,
how far did she take you? Once she'd
swum between the icy depths
between arctic coastal waters, did the
dark swills clogging the Medway
confuse her?

Were you sure of who you were, GD?
The man about town, hand
in hand with the narwhal, chasing that
unicorn dream of respectability.
In the wild, male bulls bellow and
charge. Blood flows, the damage done;
terminal.

The smarter animal
displays his teeth; a
good show nudges confrontation
to a dance. Signposted,
every one can find their place.
Oil floats above water,
if
the water stays
undisturbed.

The Buddha of Wetherspoons

The golden boy of Rochester, frequently seen
preaching to the converted in the Cathedral's shadow.
Our very own saviour floats serenely above the
sea of cigarette butts bobbing in
half-empty pint glasses.
Brilliantly blue eyes and reddish-blonde hair
spurn the light, leave an eerie after-image I blame on
dim lighting. Nobody will poach the Golden Lion –
untouchable above our cloud of stale beer and hot air,
too busy putting the world to rights
to your adoring bunch of tailors' dummies.
You are the lotus flower in our mud.
Down in the Two Brewers, some
heathens whisper about
your pinstriped suit swiped from Marks & Spencer.
But your eloquence grows over pints of cider, with ice;
there are times when I almost believe you.

Outside, normal life drops to a crawl, a whisper of fumes
and blocked exhausts. Free your chakras, play the game;
we've got to break the system from within.
Give me liberty or give me death.
Burn the zoos to the ground;
let the animals die if they can't be free. They're better off,
you know it. Don't you?
Go back to your cocoon darling;
flowers are tarts, prostitutes for the bees.
But let me buy you another round my lovely lotus blue,
while you entertain the troops,
foot soldiers in your war.
You're saving the world one soul at a time;
our Buddha of Wetherspoons.

Mama Bear

Ursula chooses not to admit; she is
out of her depth. She swims
alone through the
soft brown forest, the shaded
patches stitched

to the soft fabric of her
cheeks. In company the raft holds
firm, the seams flexing in the
tide, until the month's end when
her next injection is due.
At these times Ursula hides
deep in the cloud forest above,

resting in the cool dry of the felled
trees, the dusty paperwork that shields
the walking wounded that surround her;
the shipwrecked
and heartbroken, as they climb into the
broken branches of her refuge.
What is swimming after all, but
a refusal to sink?

Sun Pier Blue

Three cans of green; one
Carlsburg, two Zübr and
one black Pela
crumpled into wood
bleached over Chatham's
tides. The pier is blue, a
lightness never seen in
nature; regular
metalwork latticed in a
design that lingers for as long
as the sky's reflection glued to the
water's surface

I remember mustard gold
cans, a mystery special
brew. The kind knocked up by
boffins and Bond villains,
gleaming in the two dimensions
every Saturday morning while
he snored the weekday shift away

and I chewed on sour apples,
emerald caramels and gums
luminescent in black and green
emblazoned with gin, rum, cider

and a flock of black-tinged
pigeons swoop overhead in
a confusion of perspective,
nowhere near where the wind nudged
by wings slaps my face

Twenty one years today. In
the corner
closest the shore, a line of swans
circle, scatter.
A motorcycle revs, and the
sound laps at my feet across the water.

Silt up

this far out in the estuary
it was never going to be a fair fight
fresh silt washes out the salty
whore's crocodile tears
so down I went
through the liquid punctured hole
like a deft pupil
even the sharp edges of the bitch's maw
couldn't reach me here
the hydrophobia of the rabid
has some uses if your skin
lies unbroken
so many layers down
and my barbed tongue
catches on passing trails of
grey ash tapped
from the fag end of
St Mary's Island

and still I sink
past shattered corpses and carbon
dated no-named nothings
adding rings upon rings
we all fall down
to the roots buried deep
blurred daisy-chains fracture
at this depth
cobalt and asbestos
crowned dancing queens
awaiting the once and future king's
return anointing
our lady's fireproof future
invictus

untouched
untouchable
underwater
under his eye

the flounders flying high on
the grey tide like kites
announcing by their rapid
departure the arrival of the
nameless
finless and finned
come as they would
my eyes plucked and sucked dry
heart chambers ransacked
liver emptied inflamed guts wound
down untangled and
squeezed flat by passing mermaids
torn and woven
now trailing at their
throats' fresh washed scarves
coral iridescent flare sparked
in the reflection of their silver scales
as they sashay away

and yet more
gnawing at sinews until
arms drop and hips fall
at bubbled angles
like mated snails at odds
and it all settles about an empty
cage on the river's floor
and still they feed
pincers pulling
and pecking at my skull

sharp claws
scraping away
the last of the
marrow and even then
pecking at each other
until they tangle in my hair
fall away impale their fat
bellies on the
bloodied bone teeth of the
broken mermaid's comb

at the approach of high tide
my cage echoes the hum of
the Medway
softly sings the seal wife
tales of dancing barges
eclipsing the rippling heavens
clippers' rudders ripping fishing
nets open
softly sings the seal wife as she
kisses fresh water into
empty sockets
granules of sand depositing at the
gutter of tear ducts
and she disappears between the flats
and still I wait in
the arms of the tides
a liquid solution
gorged on the earth's deep veins
and veins of ore

soft falls the silt through
my bare bones
silken thin deposits form
that line empty spaces
in layers at each moon
dragged tide
four times daily
build chambers full of
stalagmites
and stalactites
graced by salt crystals
glistening jewels fit to grace a
mermaid's neck

they say water always wins

this far out in the estuary
it was never going to be a fair fight

Petalia Child

"I am a child of earth and of starry heavens"
My body remembers with each
stretch of my heart
that stirs the molten core of me,
sends heat singing out my veins;
root, branch and leaf
that radiates though my eyes,
limbs, breasts. A pulsar
beat across each solar tide,
lapping at magnetic shores.
Beached across shifting poles,
beacons calling out, like to like –
North, South, East and West
dancing in an unseen cauldron,
without borders.
Warmed in the breath of nine million
stars and their sisters, I drink,
and remember. That I am a child of earth
and of starry heavens.

*Inspired by the Petalia tablet in the British Museum. The
Petalia tablet was created around the 3rd century BCE.*

Chorus of seven

I'm the Queen of
fire, baby –
I dance it into a crown.
I can stop the world
from turning.
I can melt the ground
you walk on.
I can freeze the
heart of the world.
I have swum out to the
furthest stars and put them out.
I have resurrected
the hearts of
martyred believers.
I have turned the
turncoat out of hell.
I remember the stories
of the ones before there was
a hell, and I know the songs
of the ones that will follow you.
And I can tell you who the
martyrs are. Dare you to ask me?

Dare you to ask me
when it is to hell you go?
I am the beginning and the
end of all there was before
there was even a word,
or a last regret.
I can tell you where
this fire is going to
burn the most.

I can shimmy the
words into wounds and
scorch the breath from
your wet lungs.
Seven faces I can
show the world,
seven faces all I can show
but this one, scalded,
scales burning away.

I can set a fire into
your palate so fierce
you will do the dancing
for me.
But I cannot
stand still.

Fire in the head

The spark that ignites
the fire in my head
glows white.
Casts shadows upon the
lacquered bricks of my small cell.

The spark that ignites
the fire in my head
leapt out at me from
beneath the cauldron,
stirred by the cailleach
as she buries it in soft white ashes.

The spark that ignites
the fire in my head
scorches my tongue,
makes me dumb and
senseless to speak
of the red hot sparks fanning out like
dandelions into the cold grey waste.

The spark that ignites
the fire in my head
above my green veiny heart
stirs up the cauldron of my eye,
scalds my face.

The spark that ignites
the fire in my head
melts the adder striped
scales of my hand,
sloughs off the hard callous of
my shins and heels.

The spark that ignites
the fire in my head
heats the concrete legions
beneath Watling Street,
beneath the chalk skull crowning the soil
beneath my bended bones
and above theirs; smoking, kindling.

The spark that ignites
the fire in my head
illuminates the glorious
flood over your face
from your melted eyes.

The spark that ignites
the fire in my head
pierces my blistered tongue,
baptises the baby raw skin shining
above my restless feet,
dancing next to yours.

Heretics making a Scene on the Medway: on the occasion of William Blake's arrest.

He floats
with gentle Thomas Stothard and Ogleby,
above the jousting outlines
above the Medway,
above the seven maws of the Dragon,
before the files of disposables
marching Upnor's crooked dust
up, onto scorched foreheads –
and to dust you shall return – before
the clouds *white trailing beard* – before
the hammer, *grey hollow shell* before
the mud shaped
into bricks, baked
into numbers, stamped
into formation
in the image of god he created them.

He floats coppered points
in readiness, to draw the poison from
within the adders mouth,
blurring the chalked drenched banks
blurring away the curtain wall
blurring away the driftwood
crucified above
*and let birds fly above the earth across the vault of
the sky*
beyond the ragstone blocks
beyond the stakes sharped to splinter
beyond the sentinel spitting at the French spies
and the handcuffs haloed
around wrists.

They float, glowing fierce as fallen cherubs
wings smoked and
charred,
splayed dumb as doves.

William floats
with Albion, singing
with every child a Jesus
clothed with the sun.
God saw all that he had made, and it was very good.

*A poem inspired by the arrest in 1780 of William Blake
and two of his friends, in the belief that they were French
spies, while on a sketching trip on the river Medway.*

Seal-wife swings the delta blues

It was in the oyster beds of course;
green roots anchored deep, past where she'd
long ago stopped looking
– the shades take
more than their share –
storm-thrashed bare strands stretching
out like the song of a drowned sailor.
And she remembers him slowly;
eyes the colour of diving birds,
breath moss-dry, a crackling gust of
warmth and sound, thighs
salmon-firm, hands that
scoured like pebbles. Snail-tough
cock that reared and writhed,
waxing and waning with the tides.
His rhythmic shanties that wound around
torn weeds and crushing weights,
binding a story about leaves and branches
gasping out into nothing, torn
and burned into unnatural fancies.
She followed his words once,
winding around the curves of the Medway,
before they slipped and tangled in the waters
upstream. Charms turning in the flash frenzy
wake of boats, cutting as sharp as
the silver swimmers call,
sang to her – once – by
her mother's mother.
The one who swam
out into the Great Dark,
never came back.

Invicted

Victory
is getting out of bed, even though
it is past noon and everyone walking past
has seen that your curtains are
still closed

Victory
is having curtains in the first place,
and a net behind them, and
space to put them up and
keeping them there

Victory
is those sharp clean teeth and that cereal
that you swallow down and keep down
and the milk that is still OK to drink,
today

Victory
is remembering that above those sharp
teeth are lips that kiss, that shape
soft words:
you are allowed

Victory
is those clothes that keep you warm,
and those matching yellow socks
that remind you of
summer beaches

Victory
is making it beyond the chipped
front door today, and staying put
when they walk past, and see
right through you

Victory
is not telling them to go
fuck themselves, because really.
Who knows what their victory looks like;
is it anything like yours?

Victory
is going to bed and staying there,
not knowing if tomorrow is going to
be a victory day and
doing it anyway

acknowledgements

Works previously published

Buddha of Wetherspoons & Chicken Feed: *Anti-Heroin Chic*, October 2017

Dandelion: a declaration: *The Tree of Light: working creatively with long-term illness* 2010

GD and the Narwhal & Sun Pier Blue: *Wandering Words* online writing project

His Hands: *Beat-ITUDE National Beat Poetry Festival 10 Year Anthology* 2018

Invicted: *Please Hear What I am Not Saying* 2018

Mama Bear: *The Interpreter's House* #67

Medway Mermaid: *Unexplored Territory.* 2012

Nordkapp: *An Assemblance of Judicious Heretics: writing and art on the road not taken* 2015

Only a Fool: *Boyne Berries* #20

Seal Wife Swings the Delta Blues: *Confluence* #4

Silt Up: *Confluence* #6

Excerpts from

Foreword:
'The Song of Wandering Aengus' by W. B. Yeats

Blue tinged anchor:
'Rule Britannia' by James Thomson

.

Wordsmithery is a Medway-based independent literary arts organisation which specialises in managing literature events and projects, Literature Development, and publishing. **www.wordsmithery.info**

Find more beautifully produced, limited edition poetry and prose collections, plays and our literary magazine *Confluence*, on our website.